ANIMALS THAT HIBERNATE

LARRY DANE BRIMNER

ANIMALS THAT HIBERNATE

A First Book
Franklin Watts 1991
New York / London / Toronto / Sydney

Cover photograph courtesy of: Jeff Greenberg Agency/Sam Saylor

Photographs courtesy of: David W. Johnson: pp. 12, 55;
DRK Photos: pp. 13 (S. Nielsen), 28 (John R. Hicks), 31
(Stephen J. Krasemann), 44 (James R. Fisher), 46 (C.C. Lockwood),
48 (Johnny Johnson), 49 (Kennan Ward), 54 (John Gerlach), 56
(Wayne Lankinen), 57 (Jeff Foott); U.S.D.A., Forest Service: p. 14;
Jeff Greenberg Agency: pp. 19 (Thomas Nicastri),
24, 52 (both Thomas Henion); Paul E. Meyers: pp. 21, 35, 37, 39,
41, 42; Animals Animals: p. 26 (E.R. Degginger); Photo Researchers:
p. 32 (Merlin D. Tuttle).

Library of Congress Cataloging-in-Publication Data

Brimner, Larry Dane.
Animals that hibernate/by Larry Dane Brimner.
p.   cm.—(A First book)
Summary: Defines hibernation and describes different animals' ways
of preparing for and spending the winter.
Includes bibliographical references and index.
ISBN 0-531-20018-3
1. Hibernation—Juvenile literature. 2. Animals—Wintering—
Juvenile literature. [1. Hibernation. 2. Animals—Wintering.]
I. Title. II. Series.
QL755.B85   1991
591.54'3—dc20
90-13116 CIP AC

CONTENTS

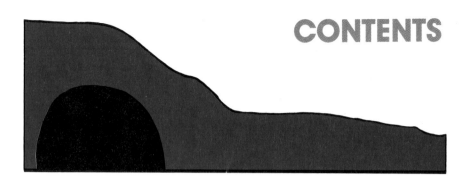

For Wayne Brimner

ACKNOWLEDGMENTS

Many people helped me with this project. I am indebted to the Natural History Museum in San Diego, California, for allowing me access to its archives and for answering my many questions. I am also grateful to the San Diego Zoo and its library staff for graciously tracking down information and never losing patience. Finally, special thanks to Dr. Lee McClenaghan of San Diego State University for generously offering his expertise and advice.

ANIMALS THAT HIBERNATE

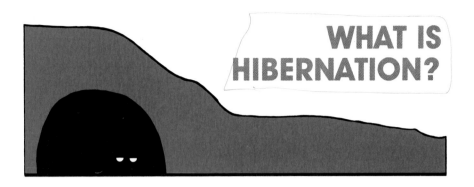

WHAT IS HIBERNATION?

What do animals do when it's winter and the weather turns cold? Some travel to warmer climates. Others undergo physical changes that help them survive cold temperatures. Another group of animals hibernates, or sleeps, during winter's most bitter weather. Animals have various ways of protecting themselves from harsh weather.

North of the equator, many animals travel, or migrate, to warmer places during the winter. Birds like robins and swallows are the migrating animals most familiar to us.

If you live near a flyway, you can see entire flocks of birds zigzagging across the sky at the end of summer and during the autumn, heading south for the winter. They may travel thousands of miles to reach their wintering places. But when warm weather returns, so do the birds. This is an instinctive cycle repeated year after year during each migrator's life.

Left: When winter arrives, the beaver has built its hut as protection against the bitter weather. Above: Canadian geese form the shape of a V in their flight toward a warmer climate.

Some animals, like the moose, don't need
to hibernate for the winter.

Some animals can be seen in the same general area all year long. They grow thicker coats of fur that protect them from the cold. The thick fur traps a thin layer of air next to the skin, which helps to insulate the animals. These animals also are protected through an extra layer of fat. This helps to prevent heat escaping from the animal's body and doesn't allow the cold to penetrate. The moose, for example, is an animal that dons thicker layers of fur and fat during the winter.

Some animals do not migrate during the winter. They are not active, either. These are the animals that hibernate during the coldest part of the year. Some hibernate for weeks at a time, while others wake after a few days. What they have in common is that sleep is their protection against winter's chill.

When an animal goes into hibernation, its body temperature drops, its heartbeat slows down, and its breathing becomes barely detectable. In this way it conserves energy. A hibernating animal enters such a deep state of sleep that it appears more dead than alive. But alive it is.

Most hibernating mammals prepare for their long winter naps by eating great amounts of food in the fall. Much of the food is stored in their bodies as fat. Later, the fat is broken down into energy. This keeps the animals alive while they are asleep and not taking in food.

In addition to regular fat, patches of a special brown fat form across the back and shoulders of hibernating animals near their brain, heart, and lungs. These are the organs that must warm up and wake up first when it's time to come out of hibernation. Brown fat sends a quick burst of energy to them. Once the brain, heart, and lungs have awakened and speeded up, the animal can send a "wake-up call" to the rest of its body.

Scientists are learning more about hibernation all the time. They know that hibernating mammals have a substance in their blood they call Hibernation Inducement Trigger (HIT). HIT goes into action when days are shorter, when there is a change in temperature, or when there is a shortage of food. They have learned that when blood is taken from a hibernating squirrel in the winter it can trigger hibernation when injected in another squirrel in the spring. But scientists do not know exactly what HIT is or exactly how it works.

Much about hibernation remains a mystery. Perhaps someday scientists will unlock all the secrets of animals that hibernate.

DEEP-SLEEPING ANIMALS

Not all hibernating animals undergo changes in their heartbeat, breathing, and temperature. Because of this, scientists disagree on whether or not all winter sleep is really hibernation. Some scientists say that the period of inactivity, or dormancy, in the bear should not be compared to the winter sleep of the woodchuck because the bear does not undergo the significant physical changes that the woodchuck does. Other scientists believe that hibernation is possible in varying degrees.

For now, some animals are called "true hibernators"; these are the deep-sleeping animals whose heartbeat, breathing, and temperature change remarkably during the winter. The other animals are sometimes called the "light sleepers." Who are the true hibernators and how do their bodies change during hibernation?

THE WOODCHUCK

Almost everyone knows about the tradition of Groundhog Day, when the groundhog supposedly comes out of its burrow on February 2 to see if the sun is shining. If it sees its shadow, it returns to its burrow to sleep through six more weeks of winter. If it doesn't see its shadow, then spring is on the way. In truth, a male groundhog leaves its burrow in February, but not to check the weather—it is looking for a mate!

In some parts of the country, groundhogs are called whistle pigs or marmots. More commonly, they are called woodchucks.

During its hibernation, the woodchuck has lived on a layer of fat stored beneath the skin. It has lost between one-third and one-half of its autumn weight. When it emerges from its long winter sleep, the animal is lean and hungry. But finding food is no easy task. The vegetation on which a woodchuck lives may not have sprouted yet, or it may still be covered with a layer of snow. The woodchuck must continue to live off its stored fat until green plants are plentiful.

From early April to mid-May, a female woodchuck gives birth to her young. She prepares for the event by driving the

Because woodchucks are active during the daylight, they can often be spotted feeding during the summer.

male from her burrow or by moving to a new one. She will give birth to a litter of four pups and care for them alone. She never allows the male near their offspring.

A baby woodchuck, or chuckling, is blind, deaf, helpless, and almost hairless at birth. It weighs only about one ounce and is less than four inches in length.

When a chuckling is about twenty-eight days old, its eyes will open. But it won't venture from its burrow until it is about six weeks old.

A female is a loving parent, but a strict one. A mother often "drills" her youngsters. Pretending to spot danger, she'll give a false alarm to make certain her pups know what to do in an emergency. A wise pup scampers into the burrow where it is relatively safe from enemies. Any pup remaining above ground is given a gentle nip. It doesn't take long for the youngsters to learn the habit of going underground when danger is present.

Because they are gnawing animals, woodchucks, like all rodents, have teeth specialized for this purpose. They have only one pair of incisors, or cutting teeth, in both the upper and lower jaw. The incisors grow throughout the animal's lifetime, but gnawing prevents them from becoming too long. During hibernation, they stop growing.

Woodchuck pups make their appearance in the spring, when food is once again available.

An adult woodchuck may weigh as much as ten pounds (4.5 kg) at summer's end. By now, young woodchucks have separated from their mother and are on their own. It is time for all woodchucks, young and old, to settle into their winter dens.

Winter quarters are dug below the frost line—the depths at which soil doesn't freeze. The entrance tunnel may slope down to a depth of five feet (1.5 m) or more, and may be forty feet (12 m) in length.

Most burrows are similar, with a main entrance around which there is a mound of dirt, a spy hole hidden in grass or underbrush, and several rooms off the tunnel, including a toilet chamber and a nest. Nests are lined with leaves and grasses, and they are placed high in the burrow so that water will not flood them.

Before the woodchuck goes into hibernation, it stops eating completely. It spends more and more time inside its burrow, only coming out to empty its bowels.

Then one day, usually in late September or early October, the woodchuck seals off part of its lower burrow by packing soil against the opening. This protects it against intruders, and since the upper tunnel isn't used by the woodchuck, it is left open and is sometimes used by rabbits, skunks, or other small animals during the winter.

Little by little, the woodchuck's body activities slow down. It rolls itself into a ball and slips into a deep sleep. The woodchuck's winter nap may last as long as six months.

During hibernation the woodchuck hardly breathes at all. In fact, it takes only about one breath every five minutes. During warmer weather, it had breathed thirty to forty times during the same interval—and as much as one hundred times a minute when excited. Instead of beating eighty times a minute, its heart now beats only four times a minute. Its temperature, which is normally about 98 degrees Fahrenheit (36.7° C), drops to about 38 degrees Fahrenheit (3.3° C), just slightly above freezing. If it should get too cold, it shivers to warm itself and wakens slightly. But once it is warm again, it returns to deep sleep.

Every so often, all hibernating animals stir during their period of sleep, and so does the woodchuck. It eats some of the food it has stored and uses the toilet chamber. Then it returns to its nest and to sleep again.

So it goes all winter. When its body clock signals, the woodchuck receives a spurt of energy from its layer of brown fat, and it starts to shiver. More oxygen is pumped to tne organs. The heart beats faster, causing more blood to circulate and the body to get warmer. In just a few hours, the woodchuck is ready to begin its seasonal cycle again.

THE GROUND SQUIRREL

North America is home to about two dozen species of ground squirrels. While not all of them hibernate, some species spend up to three-fourths of their lives asleep. One particular ground squirrel is known to have slept for thirty-three weeks without waking.

Before they hibernate, ground squirrels eat and eat and eat. As they stuff themselves, they become fatter and fatter. Accumulated fat is the source of energy these animals depend on during their hibernation and immediately after waking. If they do not become fat enough, they do not

Some ground squirrels don't drink water. The plants
they eat serve as both food and liquid.

hibernate. They receive a signal from their brains when they are fat enough.

Ground squirrels may not hibernate at all where winters are mild. But where the weather is cold, they retire to their sleeping dens and "shut their doors" by using their noses to pack loose earth into the openings.

Ground squirrels don't fall asleep all at once. A ground squirrel's bodily activities slow down little by little. The heart beats more and more slowly. The animal's breathing gradually becomes slower. Its temperature drops a little each day until it is about 40 degrees Fahrenheit (4.4° C). (Its normal temperature is about 90 degrees Fahrenheit [32.2° C].) Then it hibernates.

If the ground squirrel's temperature falls below 40 degrees Fahrenheit (4.4° C), the animal rouses slightly and increases its breathing, heart rate, and circulation. In turn, its temperature rises, preventing it from freezing to death. And like its relative the woodchuck, it wakes every three or four weeks to snack on stored seeds, then returns to a deathlike sleep.

It takes only a few hours to awaken from hibernation. Older males are the first to leave their burrows. They are extremely hungry, but there is little food available in the early spring. They eat what is left of their stored food. And they look for females because it is time to mate.

A female ground squirrel has her litter about three weeks after mating. There are between two and seven naked, blind, and toothless babies in her litter.

At birth, a baby ground squirrel weighs only about one-quarter of an ounce. It grows so quickly, though, that it sets out on its own when it is only five weeks old. It will then

repeat the cycle of its parents and be ready when hibernating time comes again.

THE JUMPING MOUSE

Another true hibernator is the jumping mouse. This small rodent makes its home in many parts of the United States and Canada.

Like the woodchuck and ground squirrel, the yellowish-brown jumping mouse concerns itself with eating and mating when it first awakens from hibernation in late April or May. Males are the first to emerge.

After mating, it takes only eighteen days for the female to have a litter of six mice. They develop so quickly that they are fully grown in only six weeks. This makes it possible for the female to have as many as three litters in one season.

When frightened, the jumping mouse usually bounds to safety. But during the summer the animal crams itself with food. As summer wears on and the jumping mouse gets fatter and fatter, long leaps become more and more difficult. The fatter it becomes, the more it is in danger of being caught by predators like hawks, owls, and snakes.

In the late summer, the jumping mouse prepares a winter den deep in the soil. No bigger than a tennis ball, the den is carefully lined with grasses and shredded leaves.

A litter of helpless baby ground squirrels, curled together for warmth.

A jumping mouse crams itself with food
during the summer. It eats seeds from grasses,
flowers, and fruits, but may also feed on
beetles, spiders, and decaying meat and fish.

When the jumping mouse waddles into its winter den for the last time, usually in October, it plugs the entrance hole with earth from the inside. It curls itself into a tight ball, with its head buried between its rear legs, and tightly wraps its tail around its thickly furred body. All of its life processes slow down, and it enters the deep sleep of true hibernation, during which it breathes only once every fifteen minutes.

 THE BAT

Many people shiver when they think about bats, not realizing that most bats actually benefit people. Using their mouths, they catch gnats, mosquitoes, moths, and other flying insects and eat them. (Only vampire bats drink blood, and they prey mostly on livestock.) Bats are the only mammals that can fly. One of the most common bats in North America is the little brown bat. It is strictly insectivorous and can eat its own weight in insects in a single night.

While some kinds of bats migrate, the little brown bat hibernates. When the temperature stops rising above 50 to 54 degrees Fahrenheit (10 to 12.2° C), swarms of little brown bats fly to their winter quarters, or hibernacula. They collect in the same caves used for centuries by their ancestors. There, the temperature doesn't change much. It remains above freezing all winter. A bat must winter in a place that remains above freezing, because when it is resting, its body temperature may become the same as that of the surrounding air. If the air is too cold, ice crystals form in the bat's blood, and it dies.

By the time it hibernates, the little brown bat has put on

layers of white and brown fat. It has doubled or tripled in weight from the one-quarter of an ounce it weighed in the spring.

When it roosts, it hangs upside down and wraps its wings around its body. Then, rapidly, its body processes slow, and the little brown bat sleeps.

A little brown bat becomes so stiff and cold during hibernation that it seems more dead than alive. Its breathing and heartbeat nearly stop. An active little brown bat breathes nearly two hundred times a minute. When hibernating, it breathes about twenty-three times a minute, and sometimes as seldom as once every five minutes. The heart of an active little brown bat beats four hundred to seven hundred times a minute. In hibernation, it beats only seven to ten times a minute.

During the winter it wakes occasionally. If there is water, it drinks, and if there are insects or spiders in the cave, it may eat. But it always returns to its hanging position and sleeps. It hibernates for three or four months, until there is a supply of early spring insects outside.

When it wakes in the spring, a bat comes out of hibernation so quickly that its temperature rises nearly two degrees per minute. And once it is fully awake, it leaves its roost and the cave to search for insects.

A swarm of Mexican fruit bats, like the little brown bats, fly out of their cave.

The Gambian epaulated bat carries its young
just as the little brown bat does.

Having mated before going into hibernation, pregnant females form nursery colonies in caves of their own, without the males.

Once the baby is born, the little brown bat mother holds the infant in her wing and nurses it at her breast. Some kinds of bats leave their infants behind while they hunt for food. But the little brown bat mother carries her baby with her. The infant clings to its mother's fur with its teeth and claws.

Soon the baby becomes too heavy for its mother. Then the mother hunts alone and returns to the roost to feed her little one. By the time the baby is one month old, it is ready to fly on its own.

The little brown bat is a nocturnal hunter, which means that it hunts at night. It is such a good hunter that it can fly at night and catch insects even when it is blindfolded. The mystery of how bats do this was solved by a scientist named Donald R. Griffin in the 1930s. He discovered that bats send out sounds that are so high pitched, human beings can't hear them. When the sounds strike an object, the bat hears the echo and is guided by it. This is called *echolocation,* and works as a kind of built-in sonar system. This enables a bat to fly at night, and is also how it captures flying insects. If a bat's ears are plugged, it crashes into everything in its path!

Like the other true hibernators, the little brown bat spends its spring and summer gobbling up food. When the temperature turns cool, the cycle begins again.

LIGHT-SLEEPING ANIMALS

Not all hibernating animals hole up for the entire winter. Instead of sleeping for months at a time, some animals go into a "winter lethargy." This means that they become sluggish and drowsy during winter's most severe weather. But as soon as it warms up again, they wake and scamper about in search of food.

 THE EASTERN CHIPMUNK

The eastern chipmunk is a light sleeper. Its scientific name is *Tamias striatus*, which means "striped storer." This is an appropriate name since the chipmunk does not store up much fat before its naps. Instead, it stores food in special storage chambers in its burrow.

*The industrious and friendly eastern chipmunk
rushes around collecting seeds and acorns,
which it will stash away as summer's end draws nearer.*

The chipmunk's frantic search for food slows near the end of summer. Near-freezing temperatures and the urge to nap arrive at the same time. The chipmunk retires to a sleeping chamber and curls itself into a tight ball on a bed of dried leaves and grasses.

Food is always handy. Not only has the chipmunk packed food into its storage chambers, but it has also built its nest on top of a store of goodies. When it wakes, all it has to do is reach under its bed for a snack.

Unlike its relative the woodchuck, the chipmunk wakes often during the winter. It has a snack, and may use the toilet chamber, the room at the deepest part of the burrow. Then it returns to sleep. If it isn't too cold, the chipmunk might slip outside. But it returns to snuggle in its nest as soon as the weather turns cold again.

Males are usually the first to get up and out, usually in late February or early March. Like the other animals that hibernate, its first urge is to eat and drink. Then it seeks out a mate.

About one month after mating, the female chipmunk has a litter of two to five helpless babies that grow up quickly. Their eyes are open by the time they are four weeks old; when they are about three months old, they brave the outside world.

Eastern chipmunks use their cheeks as storage chambers until they can take their food to their underground homes.

Soon the young chipmunk is on its own. It finds just the right spot and begins to dig its own burrow. Instinct tells it to lay in a supply of food. At the first sign of cold temperatures, it will be ready to snuggle in its nest.

THE SKUNK

When the thermometer drops below 50 degrees Fahrenheit (10° C), for several days, a skunk gets drowsy and retires to a winter den. In places where the winter is usually mild, its winter den may be temporarily borrowed from a woodchuck or other animal. But in colder places, the skunk's winter den is dug below the frost line at a depth of six to twelve feet (1.83 to 3.66 m). There, a nest of dried leaves and grass makes a soft, cozy bed for its winter sleep. Skunks usually live alone in the summer, but during the winter several may huddle together in one nest to keep warm.

There are several types of skunks. The most common is the striped skunk. It is most active at night, and can often be seen raiding garbage cans or hunting for mice. The skunk eats just about anything, plant or animal.

The scientific name for the striped skunk is *Mephitis mephitis*, which in Latin means "noxious exhalation," or "bad odor." At the base of its tail are two scent glands. If the animal is provoked, it lowers its head and raises its tail in warning.

The sometimes offensive-smelling skunk raises its tail in warning.

It may even stamp its feet to frighten away the enemy. If the threat persists, however, the striped skunk quickly turns its back on its foe and discharges a fine, oily spray from its scent glands. This drives away even the most persistent pest. And it can strike a target up to 4 yards (3.66 m) away!

A young skunk is the first to enter the winter den. As the temperature drops, the adult female is the next to arrive. The last to retreat is the adult male.

Unlike the body temperature in a true hibernator, a skunk's body temperature drops only slightly during its winter nap. Its breathing slows, but the animal can wake up easily.

Some skunks nap for as little as two weeks, and some not at all. Others stretch their winter sleep out for as long as twelve weeks. Weather is the deciding factor—when the temperature is warm, skunks are up and out.

Mating takes place at the end of winter. Nine weeks after mating, a litter of four babies is born. Like other mammal offspring, baby skunks are helpless. Their mother nurses and cares for them. Though their scent glands begin to function when they are a month old, they remain with their mother until they are about one year old, when they are ready to begin life on their own.

THE RACCOON

Like skunks, raccoons are omnivorous, which means they eat just about anything. Chiefly nocturnal, they raid garbage cans and dumps, campsites, and cabins. But this "masked bandit" also eats acorns, fruit, fish, frogs, and whatever else is available.

*This litter of four skunk babies is totally helpless
and dependent on the mother to take care of them.*

Throughout history, the raccoon has had many names. The Algonquian Indian name for the raccoon was "arakun," which means *he scratches with his hands.* In the 1700s, it was given the scientific name *Ursus lotor,* which means "washing bear." But the raccoon is not a bear. Today, scientists call the raccoon *Procyon lotor. Lotor* means "the washer," and aptly describes the raccoon's frequent habit of washing its food. Scientists believe that a raccoon's keenest sense is its sense of touch. It is thought that the washing process enables the raccoon to more easily swallow its food, because raccoons don't produce much saliva. The word *Procyon,* however, means "before the dog." This part of the scientific name is a mystery since the raccoon has no more connection to the dog than it has to the bear. The raccoon is in a family by itself. Still, the name has stuck.

The raccoon is native to the United States and its close neighbors. It can be found where there are trees and water. It often dens in the hollow of a tree, but if a good hollow cannot be found it might select an attic or a drainpipe, or might even move into the burrow of a woodchuck.

In the fall the raccoon becomes a glutton. A sixteen-pound raccoon can eat as much as three to four pounds of food a day, or one-quarter of its own weight. If a one-hundred-twenty-pound man were to eat one-quarter of his own weight in a day, he'd have to eat thirty pounds of food!

Raccoons adapt to their environment and eat whatever it has to offer.

*The mother raccoon is careful to keep her
nursing young away from the male raccoon.*

THE GRIZZLY BEAR

Anyone who has ever looked at the California state flag has seen the likeness of a grizzly bear. Part of the brown bear family, it is the largest land carnivore, or flesh-eating animal, in the world.

The territory of the grizzly once ranged from central Mexico in the south to Alaska in the north, and from the Pacific coast to Hudson Bay. Today the grizzly exists south of the Canadian border, chiefly in Yellowstone and Glacier national parks. It disappeared from California sometime in the 1920s.

Grizzlies vary in color from blond to dark brown to black. The outer fur is frosted, or *grizzled*, with gray, hence the name "grizzly." Unlike other bears, the grizzly's face is saucerlike, and there is a pronounced hump over its shoulders. And an adult male can weigh in at one thousand pounds (about 450 kg) or more!

Much of the waking part of a grizzly's life is spent in search of food. Like other bears, the grizzly is a big eater and will eat just about anything—berries, grasses, roots, bulbs, squirrels, and mice. It is an expert fisherman, often fishing streams teeming with salmon.

Although grizzlies have keen eyesight, they rely chiefly on their senses of smell and hearing to stalk their prey. They appear to be slow and clumsy, yet they can move with cat-like quickness when necessary.

Grizzlies mate in the spring. The female grizzly carries the undeveloped embryo through the summer and fall. The embryo doesn't begin to develop until after the female dens for the winter. Then, during January or February, while the

The catlike swiftness of the grizzly is useful in catching a meal.

*Although these bear cubs are no longer
helpless, they may remain with their mother until
the third summer after they are born.*

female is in a drowsy state, from one to three grizzly cubs are born.

At birth, a grizzly cub is about the size of a rat. It is blind and helpless. The mother grizzly nurses it until winter is over and it is time to leave the den.

The cub can remain with its mother until its second or third summer. There is much to learn about survival. As long as the cub and mother are together, the mother does not mate.

By August, the grizzly has begun preparing a winter den in a place where deep snow will cover the entrance. It uses its long, strong claws to dig a chamber six or seven feet (1.8 to 2.1 m) across and as much as nine feet (2.7 m) high. The entrance tunnel is sometimes as long as twenty feet (6.1 m). In the chamber, the grizzly builds a "nest" of dried leaves, grass, and twigs. Where winters are long and severe, the grizzly settles into its comfortable winter den in October.

The winter sleep of the grizzly is not a deep state of hibernation. It can awaken almost instantly to defend itself, which many true hibernators cannot. Warm weather may also interrupt the napping process. And like other bears, a grizzly may not den at all during a mild winter or where the weather isn't severe.

The true hibernators' body temperatures drop dramatically; a grizzly's changes only slightly. Grizzlies differ from true hibernators in another way, too. Grizzlies don't have to eat, drink, or use the toilet during their entire sleep—and they may spend up to six months napping!

The grizzly remains safe and snug in its winter den until it is time to begin the process again.

OTHER ANIMALS THAT HIBERNATE

Mammals are not the only animals that hibernate. The Hopi Indians told a story about a bird they called "The Sleeping One." But it wasn't until 1946, when Dr. Edmund Jaeger found a poorwill sleeping in a small pocket in a granite canyon wall, that scientists believed in the existence of a hibernating bird. The poorwill spends the cold months in a deathlike sleep in its protective pocket, then returns to its regular activities when the spring sun warms the canyon wall.

A hummingbird can zip through the air at an amazing sixty miles per hour (96.6 kph). But in the process, it uses a lot of energy. Since it can't store extra fat as a fuel source, the hummingbird enters a short dormancy. Each night, when it returns to its nest, the hummingbird shuts down its body systems to conserve energy. Then with the coming of the sun, it slips back into its high-speed life.

The small, brightly colored hummingbird's wings
beat so rapidly that they appear as a blur.

Cold-blooded animals—like frogs, turtles, and snakes—have no way to warm themselves from within. So they need to find other ways to protect themselves from cold weather.

✍ Like other animals that hibernate, frogs increase their eating in the autumn in preparation for their winter sleep. Then, when the air temperature dips toward freezing, they bury themselves by digging burrows in the muddy bottoms of ponds. The mud protects them from the colder air temperature. While they are hibernating, they take in oxygen through their skin instead of their lungs. This is possible because of air trapped in the mud. In the spring, when the sun warms the mud, the frogs begin to croak once more. Their song attracts a mate, and they begin their yearly cycle again.

During cold weather, snapping turtles and other water turtles bury themselves in mud, too. Like frogs, they get enough oxygen from the air that has been trapped in the mud. By being buried alive, they survive from one year to the next.

When they emerge in the spring, male and female snapping turtles mate. By early summer, the female is ready to lay her eggs. She comes out on land and deposits her eggs in a shallow nesting hole. As she leaves the nest, she packs the earth down over the eggs, providing them with warmth and some protection. The female turtle returns to the water and only leaves it to bask in the sun. When the next summer arrives, she leaves the water to lay her eggs again.

In eighty to ninety days, snapping-turtle eggs hatch. The young snappers immediately make their way to the water. In the water they build up the fat needed for hibernation before this cycle begins.

A male green tree frog inflates its
bubblelike vocal sacs to call a female.

*Like the frog, the snapping turtle buries
itself under mud and debris to survive the winter.*

The female snapping turtle leaves
the water to lay her eggs on land.

*Once winter is over, rattlesnakes come out
of hibernation to sun themselves.*

The rattlesnake is a cold-blooded reptile like the turtle. Found only in the Americas, rattlesnakes are pit vipers and all pit vipers are poisonous. They are called pit vipers because of the pit in each cheek. Each pit is used to sense warm objects. This is how pit vipers detect and hunt their prey.

In August or September, female rattlesnakes give birth to their young. Rather than being hatched from eggs like many snakes, baby rattlesnakes are born alive. Mother snakes do not care for their young, but the young arrive with the necessary instincts to survive. Like all snakes, they are carnivorous, and one of their first tasks is to find food.

Not long after their birth, it is time to hibernate. No one teaches them about hibernation—they hibernate by instinct. Instinct also leads them to the same place that generations of their ancestors have used as a wintering place. There, they coil with hundreds of other rattlesnakes until warm weather returns.

We cozy up to a fire or bundle up in jackets to warm ourselves during the winter. But nature provides animals with their own mysterious ways of adjusting to cold weather. Hibernation is one of those wonderful mysteries.

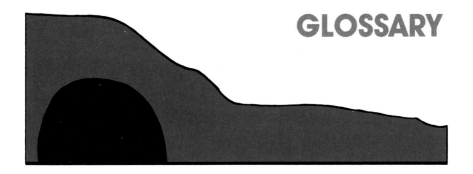

GLOSSARY

Carnivorous—flesh-eating.

Dormancy—a period of inactivity or rest.

Echolocation—locating an object through reflected sound.

Embryo—an organism in the earlier stages of development.

Flyway—an air route taken by birds during migration.

Frost line—the depth at which soil no longer freezes.

Hibernacula (singular: *hibernaculum*)—winter quarters.

Hibernation—to spend the winter in sleep.

Incisors—teeth adapted for cutting.

Insectivorous—insect-eating.

Instinct—a natural pattern of activity.

Insulate—to protect from losing heat.

Lethargy—the state of being drowsy or sluggish.

Migrate—to move from one location to another.

Nocturnal—active by night.

Omnivorous—both flesh-eating and plant-eating.

Predators—animals that hunt other animals.

Prey—an animal hunted for food.

Roost—to settle for rest or sleep; also, a place for rest or sleep.

FURTHER READING

Busch, Phyllis S. *The Seven Sleepers*. New York: Macmillan, 1985.

Chace, G. Earl. *Rattlesnakes*. New York: Dodd, Mead, 1984.

Facklam, Margery. *Do Not Disturb*. San Francisco: Sierra Club Books, 1989.

Florian, Douglas. *Discovering Frogs*. New York: Charles Scribner's Sons, 1986.

Freedman, Russell. *Rattlesnakes*. New York: Holiday House, 1984.

Lavine, Sigmund A. *Wonders of Woodchucks*. New York: Dodd, Mead, 1984.

Patent, Dorothy Hinshaw. *Bears of the World*. New York: Holiday House, 1980.

Schlein, Miriam. *Billions of Bats*. New York: Lippincott, 1982.

Silverstein, Dr. Alvin. *Mice: All About Them*. New York: Lippincott, 1980.

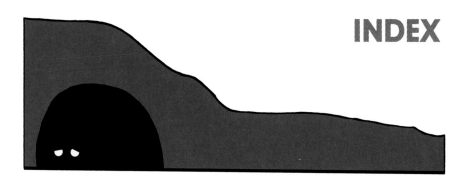

INDEX

Fat layer as insulation, 15
Flyways, 11
Food storage by hiberna-
  tors, 23, 25, 34
Frogs, 53
Frost line, 22, 38
Fur as insulation, 15

Grizzly bears, 47–50
Groundhog Day, 18
Groundhogs. *See* Wood-
  chucks
Ground squirrels, 23–27

Heartbeat during hiberna-
  tion, 15, 17, 23, 25, 30, 45
Hibernacula. *See* Winter
  quarters
Hibernating animals, 15, 16
    bats, 29–33
    bears, 17
    Eastern chipmunks,
      34–38
    frogs, 53
    grizzly bears, 47–50
    ground squirrels, 23–27
    hummingbirds, 51
    jumping mice, 27–29
    poorwills, 51
    raccoons, 40–45
    rattlesnakes, 58

skunks, 22, 38–40
turtles, 53
woodchucks, 17, 18–23
Hibernation, 11
    duration of, 15, 22, 23,
      40, 50
    interrupted, 23, 25, 30,
      34, 36, 45, 50
    physical changes and,
      15, 17, 22–23, 25, 29,
      30, 40, 45, 50
    waking from, 15–16,
      23, 25, 30
Hibernation Inducement
  Trigger (HIT), 16
Hopi Indians, 51
Hummingbirds, 51

Incisors, 20
Interrupted hibernation, 23,
  25, 30, 34, 36, 45, 50

Jumping mice, 27–29

Kits. *See* Young of hibernators

Length of hibernation, 15,
  22, 23, 40, 50
Light-sleeping hibernators,
  34–50
Little brown bat, 29–33